FROM THE BIBLE–TEACHING MINISTRY OF
CHARLES R. SWINDOLL

CHURCH FAMILY Values

INSIGHT FOR LIVING
INSIGHTS AND APPLICATION WORKBOOK

INSIGHT FOR LIVING

Church-Family Values Workbook

Charles R. Swindoll has devoted his life to the clear, practical teaching and application of God's Word and His grace. A pastor at heart, Chuck has served as senior pastor to congregations in Texas, Massachusetts, and California. He currently pastors Stonebriar Community Church in Frisco, Texas, but Chuck's listening audience extends far beyond a local church body. As a leading program in Christian broadcasting, *Insight for Living* airs in major Christian radio markets around the world, reaching churched and unchurched people groups in languages they can understand. Chuck's extensive writing ministry has also served the body of Christ worldwide, and his leadership as president and now chancellor of Dallas Theological Seminary has helped prepare and equip a new generation for ministry. Chuck and Cynthia, his partner in life and ministry, have four grown children and ten grandchildren.

Based on the original outlines, charts, and transcripts of Charles R. Swindoll's sermons, the workbook text was developed and written by the Creative Ministries Department of Insight for Living.

Copyright © 2005 by Charles R. Swindoll, Inc.

Editor in Chief: Cynthia Swindoll
Director: Mark Gaither
Editors: Greg Smith, Amy Snedaker
Copy Editors: Brie Engeler, Mike Penn
Cover Designer: Joe Casas

Original outlines, charts, and transcripts:
Copyright © 2003 by Charles R. Swindoll, Inc.

All rights reserved under international copyright conventions. No part of this book may be reproduced in any form or by any means, electronic or mechanical, including photocopying, recording, or by any information storage and retrieval system, without permission in writing from the publisher. Inquiries should be addressed to Insight for Living, Rights and Permissions, Post Office Box 251007, Plano, Texas, 75025-1007. The Rights and Permissions Department can also be reached by e-mail at rights@insight.org.

Unless otherwise indicated, Scripture references are from the New American Standard Bible®. Copyright © 1960, 1962, 1963, 1968, 1971, 1972, 1973, 1975, 1977, 1995 by The Lockman Foundation. Used by permission. (www.lockman.org)

Scripture quotations identified (THE MESSAGE) were taken from *The Message* by Eugene H. Peterson, Copyright © 1993, 1994, 1995, 1996, 2000, 2001, 2002. Used by permission of NavPress Publishing Group. All rights reserved.

Scripture quotations identified (PHILLIPS) are taken from J. B. Phillips: The New Testament in Modern English, Revised Edition. Copyright © 1958, 1960, 1972 by J. B. Phillips. Used by permission of Macmillan Publishing Co., Inc.

An effort has been made to locate sources and obtain permission where necessary for the quotations used in this book. In the event of any unintentional omission, a modification will gladly be incorporated in future printings.

Cover Image: Comstock Images
ISBN: 1-57972-667-4
Printed in the United States of America

Contents

A Letter from Chuck

If someone were to ask you how to find a good church, what would you say? Would you tell them to look for one with a good children's program, a dynamic preacher, or an innovative worship leader? Should it be a small church where everyone knows everyone else or a large church with double-decker seating? Does it need to have stained glass and a steeple or a more modern design? Or would you tell them to look beyond the programs, the size, and the style of the building and focus on the character of the people who make up the church body?

While it's tempting to choose a church for its programs, it's unwise to let programs draw you in if the character of the people behind the programs is only skin deep. When we neglect to ask essential biblical questions about the church's purpose, we can quickly find ourselves focusing on cultural styles rather than biblical substance. Rather than asking about programs, we should be asking,

"Is this church led by godly people who strive for character?"

"Does the church body honor others?"

"Do the members of this church pursue grace in their relationships?"

"Do its people seek excellence?"

"Are the leaders and members accountable to one another?"

"Are its teaching, worship, and fellowship biblically based?"

"Is this the local church God wants me to be a part of?"

The decision to join a body of believers is about far more than programs, the preacher's style, the building's size and appearance, or the worship leader's choices of music. It's about biblical essentials. Whether you're looking for a church or looking to establish a church, it's important to ask questions that lead you to the church's core values. As you examine the biblical foundations that guide good churches, you'll discover the questions you need to ask when you're looking for a good church home.

Chuck Swindoll

Charles R. Swindoll

HOW TO USE THE
CHURCH-FAMILY VALUES WORKBOOK

The *Church-Family Values* workbook is designed with three uses in mind: (1) for those serving in church leadership as they evaluate or establish a set of core values that will guide the administration of their fellowship; (2) for anyone searching for a church family by equipping him or her with knowledge of biblical standards for a church; or, (3) for those settled in a church family who want to help build their church into what God wants a church to be. Use this workbook as a tool in your personal devotions, small-group studies, or church curriculum, and discover the true nature of organized Christian community behind the politics and the programs.

Personal Devotions

Prepare your heart with an understanding of what God expects from a Christ-honoring church and its members. As you begin shaping or evaluating any church fellowship, begin with an honest look in the mirror of Scripture. Open your Bible, allow God's Word to enrich your study, and let the questions guide your journey of discovery.

Small-Group Bible Studies

Get more benefits from this workbook by sharing the experience. Combine your personal study with group discussion. You will be surprised and edified as you consider what your brothers and sisters in Christ have learned about the church.

Church Curriculum

Designate a month when each adult fellowship studies *Church-Family Values* simultaneously. Encourage and challenge one another to lay a biblical foundation for an authentic community as the Lord builds your members into a church that brings glory to God.

Every workbook chapter contains two regular features:

> ***Reflecting on His Word*** encourages you to memorize Scriptures that will transform your thinking.
>
> *A Look in the Mirror* challenges you to take a closer look at your own life and core values.

Some workbook chapters contain one or both of the following special features:

In Other Words gives you other people's perspectives on issues of leadership, character, honor, grace, accountability, and giving glory to God.

GETTING TO THE ROOT lets you tap into the original meanings of Greek words from the original text.

CHURCH FAMILY Values

1

Realistic Portrait of a Pastor

1 Corinthians 2:1–5; 1 Thessalonians 2:1–12; 1 Timothy 4:13–16

⊬⊨ ⊨⊣

Reflecting on His Word

For I determined to know nothing among you except Jesus Christ, and Him crucified.

1 Corinthians 2:2

John and Sherry sat at their dining-room table, flipping through a huge telephone book. They'd recently moved to Houston, Texas, but they still had not found a church. The problem was not a lack of possibilities. In fact, there were *too many* churches to choose from. The Yellow Pages listed hundreds of churches, all promising to be *the* best place to worship and find Christian fellowship.

John ran his fingers through his coarse black hair. "It'd take years to visit every one of these churches. Where do we start?"

Sherry sipped her coffee and nodded. "And how do we know when we've found what we're looking for?"

John chuckled. "Hey! We could just put all the names in a hat and pull one out."

Sherry rolled her eyes, then pointed at the Yellow Pages.

"Keep looking," she said.

Do you sometimes feel like Sherry and John? Finding a congregation, particularly in a large city, can be a daunting task—one that many of us have had to tackle. After all, choosing a church isn't like joining the Kiwanis Club or signing up for a bowling league. You're looking for a church family, not a club. You'll need to find a church that is strong on essentials, but also one that has strong core values.

What is the difference between *essentials* and *values*?

Essentials tell us *what* to do — ensure that worship, instruction, fellowship, and expression are biblically based.

Values describe *how* to do it — through godly leadership, character, honor, grace, excellence, and accountability.

Maybe you're not trying to find a church. Perhaps you hope to start one. As you plan a church, part of your work will be to structure the church to embody these essentials and core values. You will want to develop a strong plan for embracing the biblical essentials of worship, instruction, fellowship, and expression. You will also need to establish core values for your new church — the qualities that should be present in your congregation, your leaders, and your pastor.

You may not be looking for or starting a new church. More likely, you are part of an ongoing local church. If so, your church body is changing. Like any living organism, no church body remains the same. It is either positively building itself, maturing into Christlikeness (Ephesians 4:13–16), or it is slowly stagnating into spiritual mediocrity, perhaps even amidst much activity. The question in your case is twofold: what does God want my church to grow into, and how can I be part of that process?

It Starts at the Top

Look to the top of any enterprise and you can see why it succeeds or fails. To a very large degree, leadership determines outcome. Whether it's a Fortune 500 corporation, a professional sports team, a governing body, or a local book club, quality leadership means success; poor leadership leads to failure.

It's no different in the church. God puts a premium on quality leadership in the body of Christ. And should that surprise us? Throughout the Old Testament, the fortunes of God's people rose and fell with the state of those in charge. Likewise, when assessing the health of a prospective church — or seeking to improve your own church — you will need to consider the quality of its leadership, especially the pastor.

So you're not a pastor or an elder or serving on a pastoral search committee. Should you move on to the next church-family core value in chapter 2? Not so fast! Yes, God places a premium on healthy leadership. But isn't there a sphere in which you are a leader? Do you teach a Sunday school class? Lead a Bible study? Organize any service projects? Perform any hospitality? Lead in your home? Almost all of us operate as leaders or have significant influence in the lives of others, whether a class, a group, our children or grandchildren, or someone younger in the faith. And the qualities God looks for in a good leader are the same qualities God looks for in us. So let's press on to see what God, by His grace, calls pastors, leaders, and us to be.

The Person of a Pastor

What personal qualities should we look for in a pastor? Pastors and church leaders are people called by God to declare the truth of Christ. They are in the pulpit or in other leadership positions in the church in order to point us to Christ, not to be salesmen.

Read 1 Corinthians 2:1–5.

Godly pastors and ministry leaders understand that the person and the work of Christ deserve center stage. Verse 2 shows us that Paul made a conscious decision to abandon worldly wisdom, concentrating instead on the Lord Jesus Christ and His death on the cross.

Authentic, godly pastors follow in Paul's footsteps and model three essential qualities: *humility, dependence on Christ,* and *purity of motive.* Beware of pastors or church leaders who display overly confident or self-sufficient behavior. Leaders should be able to admit their weaknesses, tell the truth, and describe their actual feelings from time to time. If church leaders are excessively image conscious, this should raise a red flag. Every pastor and leader should *depend* on Christ and the Cross. A story often told of Charles Spurgeon says that no matter what text he chose, he moved as quickly as possible to the Cross of Jesus Christ. A pastor who embellishes theology eloquently but neglects the Cross has missed the point of the gospel!

Read 1 Corinthians 2:1–5 again. List the ways in which Paul modeled humility, dependence on Christ, and purity of motive to the Corinthians.

_____

_____

_____

_____

_____

Think about a spiritual leader you know and respect (example: a pastor, elder, Sunday school teacher, or small group leader). How does he or she model these core values?

_____

_____

_____

_____

According to verse 5, where should your faith rest?

_____

_____

_____

The Profile of a Pastor

A pastor should not only be a humble person who depends on Christ's power, but he should also manifest specific character qualities. In 1 Thessalonians 2:1–12, we see the breadth and depth of Paul's knowledge of God's truth and the candid way in which he delivered it. These verses give us a profile — both negative and positive — of what we should and should not seek in a leader's character.

Read 1 Thessalonians 2:1–6.

Four Traits Pastors Should Not Have

These verses outline four practices that did *not* characterize Paul. First, he was *not* deceptive. Consider verse 3. His words did not come from error, impurity, or deceit. Paul did not mislead people in any way. He spoke no lies. He made no empty promises. He did not twist words. Likewise, we need to look for integrity and genuine honesty in pastors and church leaders.

Read verse 5 again. Based on Paul's statement, what appears to be one reason a pastor or leader might resort to flattery?

_____

_____

Also in verse 5, Paul refers to God as the one who "examines our hearts." If you were aware of God constantly examining your heart and your motives, would that change the way you act toward others? Would you be more honest? Why?

_____

_____

_____

_____

Second, Paul was *not* a people pleaser. Paul's days of pleasing men ended when Christ entered into his life.

According to verse 4, who was Paul trying to please when he preached the gospel?

_____

_____

_____

_____

GETTING TO THE ROOT

The Greek term for *greed*, *pleonexía*, encompasses more than a hunger for money. It is a self-seeking craving of any kind, including avarice and exploitation. Greed is a quest for anything that brings self-satisfaction, growing out of complete disinterest in the well-being of others.

Listen to his words in Galatians 1:10, "For am I now seeking the favor of men, or of God? Or am I striving to please men? If I were still trying to please men, I would not be a bond-servant of Christ." Avoid pastors who grandstand in Jesus's name!

Third, Paul was *not* greedy. Paul spoke several times about those who pursued ministry for "dishonest gain." Look for honest, trustworthy pastors or ministry leaders who refuse to let greed motivate their actions. Paul says that he and his team did not minister out of greed. The love of power and affluence had no place in Paul's ministry.

Finally, Paul and those who served with him were *not* glory hogs. They were not out to promote themselves or build their own kingdoms. Ministers who are in the church for their own fame rob God of His glory. Arrogance had no place in Paul's pulpit, just as it has no room in our churches today. One of the best ways people in ministry can guard themselves from the temptation to misuse power is to cultivate a servant's heart and to invite others to keep them accountable. But that accountability must have teeth to it. The people to whom a minister submits himself must have the power to clip his wings should he stray in the wrong direction. Stay away from churches where the glory shines on anyone other than Jesus Christ.

In Other Words

Power can be an extremely destructive thing in any context, but in the service of religion it is downright diabolical. Religious power can destroy in a way no other power can. Power corrupts, and absolute power corrupts absolutely; and this is especially true in religion. Those who are a law unto themselves and at the same time take on a mantle of piety are particularly corruptible. When we are convinced that what we are doing is identical with the kingdom of God, anyone who opposes us *must* be wrong. When we are convinced that we always use our power to good ends, we believe we can never do wrong. But when this mentality possesses us, we are taking the power of God and using it to our own ends.[1]

—Richard Foster

Consider the traits to avoid that Paul lists in 1 Thessalonians 2:3–6, then try to restate them positively. For example, you might restate "not deceptive" as "honest."

Not deceptive — An effective pastor is _____ .

Not a people pleaser — An effective pastor is _____ .

Not greedy — An effective pastor is _____ .

Not a glory hog — An effective pastor is _____ .

When you examine your heart, what do you see? Do you see any of the positive characteristics in yourself? If not, how would you cultivate them (see 1 Thessalonians 2:4)?

_____

_____

_____

_____

Four Positive Character Traits

Although the four warning signs we noted are important, the absence of them doesn't alone make someone a good pastor or leader. An effective shepherd of God's flock will evidence certain positive characteristics as well.

Read 1 Thessalonians 2:7–12.

In these verses, Paul shows us four positive qualities that marked his ministry.

> *Sensitivity to needs*—An effective pastor is gentle (v. 7).
>
> *Fond affection for people*—An effective pastor is a "people person" (v. 8).
>
> *Authenticity of life*—An effective pastor is strong, but vulnerable (vv. 8–10).
>
> *Enthusiastic in affirmation*—An effective pastor is quick to encourage (vv. 11–12).

Note in verse 7 how Paul compares his manner of ministry to a nursing mother. Paul was not gruff or demanding. He was gentle. He nurtured people so that they could grow in a secure environment. Paul was sensitive to the needs of the people to whom he ministered, and he held a fond affection for them. Because of this, he was able to encourage them as he modeled a life of authenticity.

Think of a pastor or ministry leader who has greatly influenced you. What qualities did this person possess that encouraged you to grow?

_____

_____

_____

Authenticity is a quality best exemplified by someone who is unguarded, real, and open in all of his or her relationships, both inside and outside ministry contexts. Do you behave differently, or do you notice a change in your personality when interacting with those who follow you compared to your dealings with other people? If so, how? If not, how might you start modeling authenticity more?

_____

_____

_____

_____

The Priorities of a Pastor

The preceding profile lists the character traits that should be present in a pastor. However, many godly pastors have failed in ministry due to misplaced priorities. What kind of priorities should we look for in a man who is going to lead a church? Turning to Paul's letters to Timothy, we quickly see the priorities he emphasized to his son in the faith.

Read 1 Timothy 4:13–16.

Paul exhorted Timothy to guard his priorities in four distinct ways: publicly, spiritually, emotionally, and personally. A pastor's *public priorities* should include reading the Scriptures, exhorting people with the Word of God, and teaching the truths of the Bible (v. 13). In addition to public priorities, pastors and ministry leaders should maintain their *spiritual priorities* by cultivating and exercising their spiritual gifts (v. 14). A church's health is often linked to the extent to which a pastor carries out his calling according to his God-given strengths. Also, those in positions of leadership must guard their *emotional priorities* (v. 15). They are to minister with their whole hearts—to "take pains" in ministry—with a deep passion that conquers boredom, lethargy, and laziness. God calls all spiritual leaders to be enthusiastic about the work He has called them to do. Finally, pastors and spiritual leaders must frequently step up to the mirror of God's Word for a look at their *personal priorities* (v. 16).

Though most of us are not pastors, we're all called to model Christ to those who follow us. When you consider yourself—who you are as a person, the profile of your character, and the priorities of your leadership—what do you see? Take a good long look in the mirror of God's Word. Don't just glance at it and turn away. Based on the passages discussed in this chapter, are your character, your conduct, and your attitudes what they need to be?

When you thoughtfully consider your character, where are you strong? Where do you need to improve?

_____

_____

_____

_____

If someone were to imitate your conduct, would you be pleased with what you saw? What behaviors would you want to change?

_____

_____

_____

_____

If your thought life appeared in a comic strip caption over your head, how would it affect those around you?

_____

_____

_____

_____

Fortunately, our hidden thoughts do not appear for others to read, but our attitudes appear in our facial expressions, tones, and body language. If our thoughts need to be censored, we likely need to refocus our attention on Christ.

Evaluating a Pastor

When people visit a church, often their first observations focus on the pastor. Sadly, many times they use flawed criteria in their evaluation. People have been known to base their approval (or disapproval) of a pastor on everything from hairstyle and clothing to the kind of car he drives. The next time we visit a church, let's form our opinions based on the principles outlined in this chapter. Let's base our judgment on more than outward appearances by using Scripture for a more accurate assessment tool. As we keep these passages in mind, we will also be reminded to manifest the same character we expect from our pastor.

Examining Ourselves

Though most of us are not vocational pastors, all true believers in Christ are ministers of the gospel. We need to live our lives by the same standards we demand from our leaders. In other words, we should look in the same mirror we expect them to use. As God's people, we should know what we believe and why we believe it and live accordingly. If how we *live* differs from what we say we *believe*, our hypocrisy will surely offend the unbelievers we are trying to reach for Christ.

+≡≡≡+

Our ministry must be emphatic, or it will never affect these thoughtless times; and to this end our hearts must be habitually fervent, and our whole nature must be fired with an all-consuming passion for the glory of God and the good of men.[2]

— *Charles Spurgeon*

2

CHARACTER AND HONOR

Romans 12:1–2, 9–18

Reflecting on His Word

Let love be without hypocrisy. Abhor what is evil; cling to what is good. Be devoted to one another in brotherly love; give preference to one another in honor.

Romans 12:9–10

Pastor Greg Kamp left the Adkinson's house, knowing he'd probably never see the young couple again. Don and Abby had been attending Grace Fellowship Church for several months, but they recently dropped out without a word of explanation. When Pastor Greg stopped by their house for a visit, their red-faced embarrassment spoke volumes.

"It's not that we're unhappy or anything like that," Don said. "We love you. We love the people. We love your preaching. Grace Fellowship is a great church."

Abby nodded in agreement.

"It's just that your church is so small," continued Don. "We really want to go to a church that has a strong couples' ministry," Abby chimed in. "So we've decided to try out that new church across town. They have lots of activities, and we'll be able to meet hundreds of couples our own age. That's what it's all about, isn't it? Christian fellowship?"

Pastor Greg shook his head as he walked back to his car. If he had a dollar for every time he'd heard the phrase, "We love your church, but—," he'd be a millionaire. These days, people do not look for churches—they shop for them. They come with a list of features in mind, and when they find a church with the programs and activities they want, their search ends. Unfortunately, any consideration of a church's core values—the things that really define a good church in God's mind—usually comes as an afterthought, if at all.

Pastor Greg heaved a sigh and climbed into his aging car. He needed to stop by the Wilson's household before he went home. Rumor had it that they were leaving the church to join a congregation that had just built a new family life center.

Understanding Our Relationship to the World

Most of us are familiar with the adage, "Christians should be in the world and not of the world." We may even have these words memorized, stenciled on a wall hanging, or painted on a magnet on the refrigerator door. But, do we really know what it means to live in this world without letting it distract our hearts from God? Although this is important in all areas of the Christian life, living this motto is especially important when we're looking for a church or planning to start one. If we as Christians do not correctly understand our place in this world, our decisions will be based on society's values, not God's.

Because Jesus knew that the devil would use the frills of the world to attempt to woo His disciples away from God, He prayed in John 17:15, "I do not ask You to take them [Christians] out of the world, but to keep them from the evil one." First John 5:19 tells us, "We know that we are of God, and that the whole world lies in the power of the evil one." In other words, we are aliens on this planet, living in enemy territory.

Take a moment to read 1 Peter 2:9–12. How should the fact that believers are God's "royal priesthood" and "aliens and strangers" in this world affect our attitudes about ourselves? About our world? What do these verses call us to do as a result of our identity in Christ?

_____

_____

_____

_____

Sadly, many Christians cope with living in enemy territory by keeping a low profile. They live by their principles as best they can until obedience becomes inconvenient, or makes them look strange to the non-Christians around them. But God has called us to follow another way. Though we live in a world that alienates itself from the Lord, we must choose to walk with Him while we're here—and do it boldly. How can we do that? How can we live differently? Romans 12:1–2 teaches us:

Therefore I urge you, brethren, by the mercies of God, to present your bodies a living and holy sacrifice, acceptable to God, which is your spiritual service of worship. And do not be conformed to this world, but be transformed by the renewing of your mind, so that you may prove what the will of God is, that which is good and acceptable and perfect.

GETTING TO THE ROOT

The Greek word translated "transformed" in Romans 12:2 is *metamorphoō*, which means to change the essential nature of something and usually refers to its *outward* appearance. In other words, as a result of the renewing of our minds, we should begin to act very differently than the world in which we live.

Presenting Ourselves to God

Paul's words in verse 1 may sound familiar to you. It is one of the best-known verses in the Bible. Unfortunately, because it usually frightens us, it is also one of the least observed. As believers, the Holy Spirit has taken up residence within us and we have been given a new nature—a nature that wants to submit to God. However, we also retain an old mind-set bent on sin. Therefore, the act of consecration—presenting our bodies to God as a living and holy sacrifice—feels very unnatural. "Unnatural" because it is completely contradictory to our old way of thinking and living. It is not that we have tried that kind of submission and found it wanting but that we have chosen to leave it untried! Notice Paul's language in Romans 12:1–2. He is neither casual nor passive. He is urging us, pleading with us, begging us to give our whole selves to God for His purposes.

Unfortunately, we encounter at least three problems when we try to place our whole selves at God's disposal.

- *We are living rather than dead.* The problem with a living sacrifice is that it tries to crawl off the altar when things get hot! As living sacrifices, we must willingly choose to follow Christ, especially when the pain becomes intense.

- *We live in an unholy world.* The choices we make when we're concerned about pleasing God will look dramatically different from decisions made based on the cultural messages most people follow. When we follow His leading, we deliberately set ourselves apart unto Him.

- *We live in tension with our culture.* When we set ourselves apart to God, we must make choices and decisions based on what pleases God. Unbelievers will often reject our values and priorities, and we must accept that we will be misunderstood.

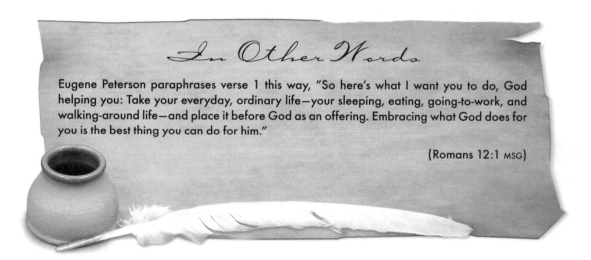

In Other Words

Eugene Peterson paraphrases verse 1 this way, "So here's what I want you to do, God helping you: Take your everyday, ordinary life—your sleeping, eating, going-to-work, and walking-around life—and place it before God as an offering. Embracing what God does for you is the best thing you can do for him."

(Romans 12:1 MSG)

Because we belong to God, our choice to present our bodies to Him as living sacrifices is the essence of worship. We're saying, "Here I am, Lord. Use me as You will for what You will. I give You all of me as a tool to be used by You for your purposes. If You call me to change my behavior, I will change my behavior. If You ask me to suffer to let others see You, I accept the pain. If I need to let go of something to embrace You, I will, by Your grace, release it to Your care." When we approach our lives with this mind-set, our choices and desires will be dramatically different. And when we look for a church or seek to start one, we will be thinking about values—not programs and activities—because we have presented and dedicated ourselves first to God. This new mind-set is what Paul means when he talks about being transformed.

Renewing our Minds

The kind of consecration to which Paul calls us in Romans 12:1 requires the radical transformation described in verse 2. Rather than being *conformed* to this world, we're to be *transformed* by God's Word. The Bible is the primary means by which God communicates with us. He reminds us of His purposes, His character, His plans. To be transformed by it, we must read it, study it, memorize it. God's Word is alive and active and immensely powerful (see Hebrews 4:12–13). Therefore, renewing the mind is no surface change. No touch-up job. The transformation is a major overhaul from within! By fixing our full attention on God and receiving our direction from His Word and prayer, we're changed from the inside out.

If we are truly Christ-followers, our values will grow to be radically different than those of others around us. And those values will affect both how we live and how we look for a church.

What core values should followers of Christ embrace?

Character in ourselves

Honor to others

Grace in our relationships

Excellence in our pursuits

Accountability to others

Glory to our God

Embracing Core Values

If programs, buildings, and other such external trappings are not to be our primary criteria for choosing a church, what should we look for? Obviously, as mentioned in chapter 1, we should seek a church that is strong on the essentials: biblically based worship, instruction, fellowship, and expression. However, we shouldn't stop there. We need to look for a church whose leaders and members embrace a set of core values that reflect transformed minds and hearts.

Different churches and people may express them differently, may call them by different names, and may even list more values than are enumerated here. But among true followers of Christ, certain values will be upheld. How can we know if a particular congregation has embraced these values? The best way to recognize them in others is by embracing them ourselves.

Character in Ourselves

Followers of Jesus Christ should be people of character, people of integrity. What is integrity? It is dealing with every person and situation in our lives with complete, loving honesty. It is living without hypocrisy. It is refusing to have different standards for different situations. If we are people of integrity, we are so committed to living in harmony with truth that we don't change our words when the boss has left the room. We don't act one way at church on Sunday and a different way with our Friday-night buddies. We refuse to tell our kids, "Do as I say, not as I do." We display consistent character qualities all the time, with everyone, and in every situation. We are people who strive to reflect God's glory and who ask Him to wipe away the smudgy parts of our life that blur His image.

Can the world see Jesus clearly in you? Honestly consider the following questions:

1. Do you do what you say you will do when you say you will do it?

A) Always   B) Usually   C) Sometimes   D) Seldom

2. Do you honor your financial obligations in a timely manner?

3. If your children or others close to you could only watch your actions rather than listen to your words to learn your values, would their observations be consistent with what you say you value? Ask them and see if you are right.

4. Can you be trusted not to hurt a friend or blame another person in order to protect yourself?

5. Do you bend the truth when it's convenient? Ever?

6. If all the people with whom you live, work, play, and go to church were in a room talking about you, how would they describe

you? Would they describe you as a person of character? If not, what do you think would be the first topic of conversation?

_____

_____

We may find leaving integrity at the door especially tempting when we walk into the business world. After all, business is business. And, to get ahead, we have to play hardball, right? Think again. Integrity in the workplace or marketplace is just as important as it is at home or in church. Good character is not something we can put on and take off as it suits us. We either wear it all the time or not at all. If we find ourselves varying our character according to setting, we can be certain that we are not pursuing Christlikeness. Say no to sending double messages. Remember, the masks of a hypocrite are always changing but an honest man's face stays the same.

Read Psalm 15, then answer the following questions about the character (integrity) of a godly person.

According to verse 2, who is the person who will live in God's tent?

_____

Verses 3–5 list some practices and qualities of the person of integrity. List them in the space below.

_____

_____

_____

_____

Would it make you uncomfortable if your friends were to hear everything you say about them when they are not around (see verse 3)?

_____

Are you honest about your finances? Do you pay people what you owe them? Do you work as hard for your employer as you would want someone you hired to work for you?

_____

Honor to Others

Becoming a person of integrity carries with it a great temptation to become proud. This leads to the second core value that every believer in Christ should embrace: *honor to others.* In Romans 12:3, we are reminded not to think too highly of ourselves. Rather than growing puffed up as we strive to be more like Christ, we're to remember that all of our integrity results from God's grace. If we forget this essential truth, it is easy to feel proud and become self-serving. Instead, we should realize the importance of all believers in Christ and honor them above ourselves. How do we do that? In Romans 12:9–18, Paul gives us a grocery list of ways we can cultivate the practice of honoring others.

> Let love be without hypocrisy. Abhor what is evil; cling to what is good. Be devoted to one another in brotherly love; give preference to one another in honor; not lagging behind in diligence, fervent in spirit, serving the Lord; rejoicing in hope, persevering in tribulation, devoted to prayer, contributing to the needs of the saints, practicing hospitality. Bless those who persecute you; bless and do not curse. Rejoice with those who rejoice, and weep with those who weep. Be of the same mind toward one another; do not be haughty in mind, but associate with the lowly. Do not be wise in your own estimation. Never pay back evil for evil to anyone. Respect what is right in the sight of all men. If possible, so far as it depends on you, be at peace with all men.

These ten verses can really change attitudes and actions! When we embrace them as core values, we will:

- Love honestly, without hypocrisy (v. 9).

- Live with discernment, holding on to good and rejecting evil (v. 9).

- Devote ourselves to each other (v. 10).

- Give preference (show respect) to others in honor (v. 10).

- Serve others diligently and with enthusiasm (v. 11).

- Be a people of hope, perseverance, and dependence on prayer (v. 12).

- Show generosity and hospitality to others (v. 13).

- Love our enemies (v. 14).

- Empathize with those who mourn, and celebrate with those who rejoice (v. 15).

- Be humble enough to associate with people of all colors and social strata (v. 16).

- Show respect to—and try to be at peace with—everyone (vv. 17–18).

We will treat people in a godly way because these are our core values. These are the things followers of Jesus Christ consider important.

When we fail to honor others above ourselves, we lose our voice because we look just like the rest of the world. If we can't show genuine love to everyone—Christians and non-Christians alike—why should the world believe our message of love? When we live our lives in such a way that the world sees the authenticity of our character and the way we honor others in love, they will see the difference that Christ makes.

Living It Out

Do we consider ourselves to be representatives of Jesus Christ in all that we do? Does the watching world see something different in us? Consider the excellence Howard Hendricks encountered while traveling home on a plane that was delayed for six hours. Even though the flight crew was not responsible for the delay, one disgruntled passenger chose to take out his frustration on a flight attendant. Dr. Hendricks walked back to the galley to talk to her and said:

> "You know, I'm a frequent flyer, and I'm always looking for somebody doing a good job. American Airlines should be proud to have you on the team. I cannot believe how nicely you handled this obnoxious character sitting across from me."

> She smiled and said, "Thank you very much."

> Then I asked, "Could I have your name? I would like to write the company and tell them how much I appreciate you."

> "Oh," she said, "I wouldn't. You need to know that I don't work for American Airlines."

> "Oh, really?"

> "No, I represent the Lord Jesus Christ."[1]

All true believers in Jesus are His representatives in this world. If we are to be effective as His agents, we must be people of character, and we must seek to honor others above ourselves. As we embrace those values, we will be better able to recognize—or form—a church that embodies them. Unlike the couple mentioned earlier in the chapter, we'll view church programs as extensions of the heart of the church—as places where we can serve rather than be served.

＋═══＋

Work from the heart for your real Master, for God, confident
that you'll get paid in full when you come into your inheritance.
Keep in mind always that the ultimate master you're serving
is Christ.

—Colossians 3:23–24 MSG

3

GRACE IN ACTION

Selections from Ephesians 2 and Romans 14

Reflecting on His Word

Therefore let us not judge one another anymore, but rather determine this—not to put an obstacle or a stumbling block in a brother's way. . . . So then let us pursue the things which make for peace and the building up of one another.

Romans 14:13, 19

"I don't think I want to go to church today," Philip told his wife, Carol. "In fact, I'm not sure if I ever want to go to church again."

Philip and Carol had been married six months, and for the most part, they were happy. But church attendance was becoming an increasingly sore spot in their relationship. At first, Philip had agreed to join Carol's home church, even though he had been raised in a different denomination. They both loved Jesus, and Carol's pastor definitely preached the Bible. The church did have a lot more rules than Philip was used to, but now that he was getting married, he thought a more disciplined lifestyle would be good for him. However, over time Philip became disillusioned with the church, its leaders, and even his own faith.

Carol didn't understand at all.

"Philip, we are expected to be there any time the doors are open," she said. "You know that."

Philip sat back in his recliner, his eyes red and watery. His jaw muscles worked as he fought to keep his emotions under control. He shook his head. "I'm tired, Carol. Tired of being expected to live up to a bunch of rules that I never accepted in the first place. I used to enjoy being a Christian. Now, I wonder . . . ." Philip put his head in his hands and said no more.

Carol went to church alone that Sunday.

Toxic faith is a real phenomenon. Whether it comes from legalism, a judgmental or oppressive church environment, or self-serving hypocrisy in leadership, toxic faith is a spiritual poison that drains people, abuses them, and discards them like trash. It often produces cynics who reject the faith they once embraced. And, when toxic faith is not producing cynics, it is cloning itself in the people it oppresses, creating carriers—people who spread the poison of legalism and judgmentalism wherever they go.

In his book *Toxic Faith*, Stephen Arterburn tells the story of his grandmother who in faith gave almost half of her modest income to various ministries because she wanted people to know Christ. Sadly, some of the people she supported took the money for their own gain rather than using it for the cause of Christ. These leaders who claimed to be champions of the gospel turned out to be charlatans. Arterburn writes:

> These unfaithful human beings who spent Nany's money had more faith in themselves than they did God. They relied more on their manipulations than on God's providence. They were more concerned about their own comforts than the people that gave them money or the people the money was intended to help. They built big empires for themselves while my grandmother turned off her heater at night to save money in order to give more. Their faith was toxic.[1]

Manufacturers put caution labels on bug sprays, fertilizers, and cleaning products to protect us from them. Parents install childproof locks on cabinets to keep curious little ones away from them. But we won't find a warning sign on the doors of churches that injure people. Ministers who mistreat their congregations have learned how to provide the scent and the feel of God, but their leadership lacks God's authentic touch and awesome presence.

Genuine—even prominent—Christians can be poisoned by toxic faith. Paul wrote the book of Galatians to address a problem of poisonous teaching. Some people were teaching that, in addition to believing in Jesus, a person had to be circumcised and keep the Jewish law to be saved.

Read Galatians 2:11–14, then answer the following questions.

What two well-known Christians were temporarily poisoned?

_____

What did they do that demonstrated toxic faith?

_____

What did Paul do when he saw the hypocrisy of these two believers?

_____

When we're seeking a church, or planning to start one, we need to safeguard ourselves against practitioners of toxic faith. We build those safeguards by operating from a set of biblical core values. These values, which include character in ourselves, honor to others, grace in our relationships, excellence in our pursuits, accountability to one another, and glory to God, will keep our roots firmly planted in God's Word. The result will be healthy, wholesome fruit—fruit that is life-giving, not poisonous. Although all of the values mentioned above will protect us against toxic faith, the most important value in facing this problem is practicing grace in our relationships.

What core values protect us against toxic faith?

Character in ourselves

Honor to others

Grace in our relationships

Excellence in our pursuits

Accountability to one another

Glory to our God

Understanding Grace

How does grace protect us from the poison of legalism and judgmental attitudes? To learn the answer to that question, we must understand how grace brings us into a relationship with God. Ephesians 2:1–10 explains in detail how God's grace works in a Christian's life.

> And you were dead in your trespasses and sins, in which you formerly walked according to the course of this world, according to the prince of the power of the air, of the spirit that is now working in the sons of disobedience. Among them we too all formerly lived in the lusts of our flesh, indulging the desires of the flesh and of the mind, and were by nature children of wrath, even as the rest. But God, being rich in mercy, because of His great love with which He loved us, even when we were dead in our transgressions, made us alive together with Christ (by grace you have been saved), and raised us up with Him, and seated us with Him in the heavenly places in Christ Jesus,

so that in the ages to come He might show the surpassing riches of His grace in kindness toward us in Christ Jesus. For by grace you have been saved through faith; and that not of yourselves, it is the gift of God; not as a result of works, so that no one may boast. For we are His workmanship, created in Christ Jesus for good works, which God prepared beforehand so that we would walk in them.

According to Ephesians 2:1, what is the spiritual condition of the unbeliever?

_____

Ephesians 2:2–3 describes the enslavement of a person who does not know Christ. Who controls an unbeliever's life, and what is the unbeliever's destiny?

_____

_____

_____

Ephesians 2:4–6 tells us what God did for us. Read the verses and fill in the blanks below:

God made us _____ together with Christ (v. 5).

God _____ us up with Christ (v. 6).

God _____ us with Christ in the heavenly places (v. 6).

Read verses 8 and 9. These verses tell us how a person is saved—by grace, through faith. Have you received God's gift of grace through faith in Jesus Christ? If not, you may wish to read the "How to Begin a Relationship with God" section in the back of this book.

If we are saved by God's grace, we should live by grace. God accepted us while we were dead in sin, enslaved to the world and Satan, and under God's wrath. But He did more than accept us. He raised us up from spiritual death and seated us with His Son. Grace is the favor of God that we do not deserve. If we are people of grace, we should show that same undeserved favor to everyone we come in contact with. Grace is the only way to be born spiritually, and it is the only way to live spiritually. If we live this way, we will be inoculated, so to speak, against the poison of toxic faith. We will know how to recognize and avoid legalism and judgmentalism in others and in ourselves.

Practicing Grace in Our Relationships

Practicing grace means that we are willing to let others be. In Romans 14:1–18, Paul gives us four guidelines that show us how to do this. Let's look at the truths these verses reveal.

Accepting Others

> Now accept the one who is weak in faith, but not for the purpose of passing judgment on his opinions. One person has faith that he may eat all things, but he who is weak eats vegetables only. The one who eats is not to regard with contempt the one who does not eat, and the one who does not eat is not to judge the one who eats, for God has accepted him. Who are you to judge the servant of another? To his own master he stands or falls; and he will stand, for the Lord is able to make him stand. (Romans 14:1–4)

Guideline: Accepting others is basic to letting them be. The absence of judgment makes room for an acceptance motivated by love.

A controversial issue early Christians struggled with was whether or not they should eat meat from an animal that had been offered to idols. Since most of the meat in the markets came from temples dedicated to idols, this was an important issue to the early church. Some Christians, whose faith was strong, would say, "It's only a piece of meat. There's nothing wrong with eating it." Others were concerned about whether or not eating such meat would make them idolaters—so they would refuse to eat it. Paul's advice to the Christians of that day, saying not to judge, still applies to us. He said, "The one who eats is not to regard with contempt the one who does not eat, and the one who does not eat is not to judge the one who eats, for God has accepted him" (Romans 14:3).

Take a moment to think of a time when you and another believer held different convictions on an issue Scripture did not specifically address. What was the issue? Were you able to let the other person be or did you feel the need to get them to agree with you?

_____

_____

_____

_____

The key idea here is acceptance. God has accepted us by His grace; we must accept one another by that same grace. Before you wound another believer by trying to impose your convictions on them, ask yourself how you would want someone on the other side of the issue to treat you. Then, act accordingly.

Refusing to Dictate to Others

> One person regards one day above another, another regards every day alike. Each person must be fully convinced in his own mind. He who observes the day, observes it for the Lord, and he who eats, does so for the Lord, for he gives thanks to God; and he who eats not, for the Lord he does not eat, and gives thanks to God. For not one of us lives for himself, and not one dies for himself; for if we live, we live for the Lord, or if we die, we die for the Lord; therefore whether we live or die, we are the Lord's. (Romans 14:5–8)

Guideline: Refusing to dictate to others allows the Lord full freedom to direct their lives.

Just as we should not accept or reject other believers on the basis of our personal lists of dos and don'ts, we also should not seek to impose our lists on others. Rather, we should trust God to guide their lives. After all, Christ is Lord, and the pace at which He brings others into fellowship and obedience is His responsibility, not ours. Brother-bashing and sister-smashing are the favorite indoor sports of legalistic Christians. We should never act that way. We are the Lord's, and so are our brothers and sisters in Christ. Our treatment of one another should reflect our mutual dependence upon Him.

According to Romans 14:5–6, what should determine a person's conviction on a gray issue?

_____

_____

_____

_____

Freeing Others

> For to this end Christ died and lived again, that He might be
> Lord both of the dead and of the living.
>
> But you, why do you judge your brother? Or you again,
> why do you regard your brother with contempt? For we will
> all stand before the judgment seat of God. For it is written, "As
> I live, says the Lord, every knee shall bow to Me, And every
> tongue shall give praise to God." So then each one of us will
> give an account of himself to God. (Romans 14:9–12)

Guideline: Freeing others means we never assume a position we are not qualified to fill—that of being a judge.

Seven reasons we are unqualified to judge other believers:

We do not know all the facts.

We cannot read motives with certainty.

We can never be completely objective.

We cannot see the big picture.

We all have blind spots.

Our prejudices blur our perspective.

We are imperfect and inconsistent.

We are not qualified to judge our brothers and sisters in Christ. Judges need to have all the facts and to be impartial. The only one who fills these qualifications is God. So, instead of judging others, we would do well to remember that we too will stand before God's judgment seat someday.

Should we simply close our eyes to the sin we see in other believers? Not at all. Sometimes sin demands confrontation, particularly in the church. Choosing not to judge does not mean that we agree with or approve all of our brothers' or sisters' actions. It does mean that we must rein in our assumptions, weigh our thoughts, and hold our tongues on matters that are not ours to measure.

Loving Others

> Therefore let us not judge one another anymore, but rather determine this—not to put an obstacle or a stumbling block in a brother's way. I know and am convinced in the Lord Jesus that nothing is unclean in itself; but to him who thinks anything to be unclean, to him it is unclean. For if because of food your brother is hurt, you are no longer walking according to love. Do not destroy with your food him for whom Christ died. Therefore do not let what is for you a good thing be spoken of as evil; for the kingdom of God is not eating and drinking, but righteousness and peace and joy in the Holy Spirit. For he who in this way serves Christ is acceptable to God and approved by men. (Romans 14:13–18)

Guideline: Loving others requires that we express our liberty wisely.

A person who practices grace exercises liberty without flaunting it. Grace never gives us the right to rub anyone's nose in our freedom. On the contrary, we are to consider the welfare of others as more important than our own. Consider how verse 1 admonishes us to do this. We are to determine (resolve) not to put a stumbling block in a brother or sister's way by flaunting our freedom. The question is not "Who's right?" Rather, it is "What is more important—displaying your liberty or preserving your fellow Christian's welfare?"

Consider the issue of drinking alcohol. For some people, having a glass of wine with dinner would be unthinkable. For others, enjoying a beverage containing alcohol presents no moral dilemma at all. On one hand, Scripture clearly says that being drunk is wrong; however, it does not speak as clearly on the issue of total abstinence. So what should we do if we'd like to enjoy a glass of wine with our meal, and the brother or sister we're dining with believes it is wrong? Skip the wine! On the other hand, what do we do if we're the one who disapproves of drinking, but we're with a fellow Christian who has no such conviction? Do not judge them; accept them! In other words, whatever side of a gray issue we find ourselves on, we should grow up, lighten up, and let the other person be.

What can you do to make sure that you are extending grace to others rather than poisoning them with toxic faith? Whether you consider yourself strong or weak in the faith, here are four thought-provoking questions to help you put the people in your life first.

1. Read Romans 14:19. In what ways are you concentrating on things that encourage peace and assist others' growth?

_____

_____

2. Read Romans 14:20. Are you guilty of sabotaging saints and hurting the work of God by imposing your personal convictions on others? Explain.

_____

_____

_____

3. Are you exercising your liberty only with those who can enjoy it with you, or do you tend to flaunt your liberty in a weaker person's face?

_____

4. Do you find yourself holding other believers in contempt when they won't participate in an activity you believe is acceptable? Or do you find yourself condemning another believer who engages in an activity you think is wrong? Evaluate your attitude in the light of Romans 14:3.

_____

_____

_____

_____

Be firm about your own convictions. But if God does not demand those convictions in Scripture, do not require others to follow them.

Grace comes free of charge to people who do not deserve it and I am one of those people. I think back to who I was—resentful, wound tight with anger, a single hardened link in a long chain of ungrace learned from family and church. Now I am trying in my own small way to pipe the tune of grace. I do so because I know, more surely than I know anything, that any pang of healing or forgiveness or goodness I have ever felt comes solely from the grace of God. I yearn for the church to become a nourishing culture of that grace.[2]

—*Philip Yancey*

4

EXCELLENCE AND ACCOUNTABILITY, ALL FOR GOD'S GLORY

Selected Scriptures

Reflecting on His Word

Whatever you do, do your work heartily, as for the Lord rather than for men, knowing that from the Lord you will receive the reward of the inheritance. It is the Lord Christ whom you serve.

Colossians 3:23 – 24

Iron sharpens iron, So one man sharpens another.

Proverbs 27:17

For from Him and through Him and to Him are all things. To Him be the glory forever. Amen.

Romans 11:36

What do the Enron executives, Martha Stewart, and we have in common? You're probably thinking, "Not much!" Think again. Though most of us have never been multi-millionaires facing allegations of fraud, we probably have stepped on others to promote ourselves or cut corners for personal gain. Stop and think about it for a minute. Have you ever tried to impress someone else by making fun of a friend or coworker and justifying yourself with the words, "It's all in good fun"? Have you ever fiddled away your workday, acting busy when you really weren't doing much of anything? Have you ever done a project just adequately rather than as well as you could have?

When life's demands press in on us, it is easy to leave character behind. That is why it is so important to embrace a set of biblical core values that will keep us rooted in God's Word and focused on God's purpose for our lives. As these values become ingrained in our minds and hearts, they will increasingly govern—and guide—our actions, attitudes, and words. In fact, these core values will transform religious people into people who genuinely want to follow Christ and make a difference in the lives of others. Whether we're looking for a church family, planning to start a new church, or just moving along in the daily grind of life, these values will guide us in making Christlike decisions.

What core values should followers of Christ embrace?

Character in ourselves

Honor to others

Grace in our relationships

Excellence in our pursuits

Accountability to others

Glory to our God

Reviewing Core Church Values

Chapter 1 of this workbook focused on what we should look for in a spiritual leader, a minister, or a pastor. When we're looking for a church home, scriptural assessment of essential values is an important consideration. In other words, is there godly leadership and direction in the church? If there is, chances are good that the church will be strong in its other values. Chapter 2 covered two of the six biblical core values or church-family values: character in ourselves and honor to others. Reflecting God's glory begins with character and integrity. If we don't have these core values, our ministry will fall flat.

Chapter 3 called attention to the importance of showing grace in our relationships. Just as we came to Christ by grace, we should relate to one another in the same way. People need to be given room to grow and develop in their relationship with God without us trying to impose our personal dos and don'ts on them. We need to let go of our personal requirements of one another and open our hearts in acceptance of one another.

Pursuing Core Values

In this final chapter, we will focus on three additional core values: excellence, accountability, and giving glory to God. These values grow out of integrity, humility, and grace. These values will cause us to stand out in such a way that people will take notice. God will be glorified through our godly behavior.

Excellence in Our Pursuits

Excellence can be an intimidating word. It may stir up thoughts of having to be perfect. Don't make the mistake of confusing the worthwhile pursuit of excellence with a neurotic drive for perfection. Excellence is *not* obsessive. Rather, excellence is using our gifts to the fullest for His work. It is taking the time to plan well for whatever we seek to do. It is also giving appropriate attention to detail as well as scheduling enough time to perform a project thoroughly without being rushed. On the other hand, valuing excellence does not mean that we hold others or ourselves to unrealistic standards. God expects our best; He doesn't require us to be superhuman.

With God, quality is always more important than quantity. Too often churches pursue second-rate quality as though it is a virtue. Whether we call it stewardship or heavenly-minded spending, many of our buildings are monuments to mediocrity. Perhaps, more than anything, we fear the accusation that elegance and beauty are carnal and extravagant. However, anyone who believes that God does not care about beauty and excellence need only read the descriptions of the Tabernacle in the Old Testament. God cares about beauty—and about excellence.

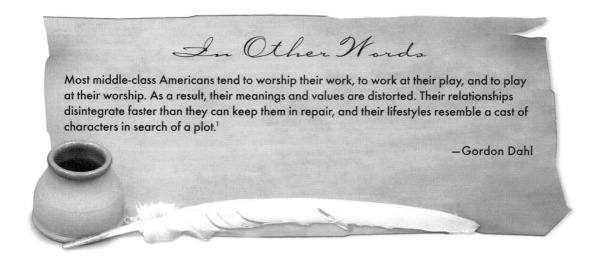

In Other Words

Most middle-class Americans tend to worship their work, to work at their play, and to play at their worship. As a result, their meanings and values are distorted. Their relationships disintegrate faster than they can keep them in repair, and their lifestyles resemble a cast of characters in search of a plot.[1]

—Gordon Dahl

When we endeavor to do something in the name of God, whether it is singing a solo, printing a worship folder, teaching a lesson, or erecting a building, our work should be the very best we can do—especially when compared to the world's standards of excellence. After all, it is God's reputation that is at stake.

Consider Paul's words in Colossians 3:15–17:

> Let the peace of Christ rule in your hearts, to which indeed you were called in one body; and be thankful. Let the word of Christ richly dwell within you, with all wisdom teaching and admonishing one another with psalms and hymns and spiritual songs, singing with thankfulness in your hearts to God. Whatever you do in word or deed, do all in the name of the Lord Jesus, giving thanks through Him to God the Father.

Notice the phrases "Let peace of Christ reign in your hearts" and "Let the word of Christ richly dwell within you." How can Christ's peace in your heart and His Word dwelling in you change your motivation when you are doing your work?

_____

_____

_____

_____

_____

_____

Look closely at verse 17. Which of the following activities does the phrase, "whatever you do in word or deed" not cover?

_____ Driving to work in rush hour traffic

_____ Working for a difficult boss

_____ Doing a project with a coworker who wants to cut corners

_____ Helping your kids with their homework

Although the preceding list may seem mundane, it emphasizes that the words "whatever you do in word or deed" should encompass every part of our lives. In everything that we put our minds and our hands to, we are to do these in the name of Jesus and with a thankful spirit.

Take a minute to think about a typical day in your life. What if you gave a business card to every person you interacted with or worked for, but instead of listing your contact information, the card simply read, "I represent the Lord Jesus Christ"? Would your words, your attitude, or your actions change? If so, how?

_____

_____

_____

_____

In Colossians 3:23–24, Paul emphasizes the attitude that produces the character trait of excellence:

> Whatever you do, do your work heartily, as for the Lord rather than for men, knowing that from the Lord you will receive the reward of the inheritance. It is the Lord Christ whom you serve.

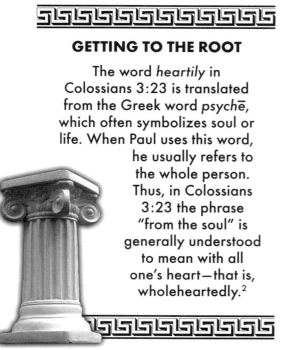

GETTING TO THE ROOT

The word *heartily* in Colossians 3:23 is translated from the Greek word *psychē*, which often symbolizes soul or life. When Paul uses this word, he usually refers to the whole person. Thus, in Colossians 3:23 the phrase "from the soul" is generally understood to mean with all one's heart—that is, wholeheartedly.[2]

Paul says in these verses that we should do our work "heartily." Literally, this reads "from the soul." It means we should approach our lives, work, and service with all our heart. Whatever we do, we should do it from the soul, not from a half-hearted commitment. If we sing, we should sing "from the soul." If we write, we write "from the soul." If we perform surgery, we perform surgery "from the soul." If we clean house, we clean house "from the soul." If we balance our checkbooks, we balance our checkbooks "from the soul." What is our motivation? What will keep us on a course of excellence? It is the knowledge that we are serving the Lord Jesus Christ. He values excellence, and He will reward excellence. In other words, our commitment to our work and the quality of the job we do come not from the perceived importance of the task but from the One we serve—the Lord Jesus Christ.

A strong standard of personal excellence will prove to be a valuable guide when looking for a church that strives for excellence. When visiting congregations, do you see quality or mediocrity? Is the church just getting by, or are the people striving to do the very best they can for the Lord Jesus? This has nothing to do with size or wealth. Pursuing excellence is all about attitude. Despite its size and wealth, a megachurch can exhibit mundane mediocrity, while a tiny congregation in the poorest part of town can display vibrant excellence—even when it is just barely able to pay the bills. What makes the difference? The attitude that says, "Whatever you do, do it heartily, as to the Lord and not to men."

On a scale of 1 to 10, with 1 signifying just getting by and 10 being wholehearted, how would you describe your attitude toward the work you do at the office? In your family life? At your church? Explain.

_____

_____

_____

_____

Accountability to Others

Perhaps the most neglected core value is accountability to others. Every time a well-known pastor or national ministry leader falls, the downfall serves as a sober reminder that no one is immune to moral failure. Everyone faces temptation—the variety is endless—but few have formulated a plan to deal with it. The result, despite our good intentions and resolve to live for Christ, is that we fall.

Why do some people yield to temptation while others are able to successfully resist it? In a word—*accountability*. Christians who have given other believers access into the secret areas of their lives are more likely to stand firm in the face of temptation. Conversely, believers who isolate themselves from others run into trouble.

If anyone could have claimed the right to keep his life private and not be accountable, the apostle Paul would certainly qualify. Yet he was willing to open his life to the scrutiny of other believers. Consider Colossians 4:7–9:

> As to all my affairs, Tychicus, our beloved brother and faithful servant and fellow bond-servant in the Lord, will bring you information. For I have sent him to you for this very purpose, that you may know about our circumstances and that he may encourage your hearts; and with him Onesimus, our faithful and beloved brother, who is one of your number. They will inform you about the whole situation here.

Don't miss Paul's accountability to the people he served with. Paul didn't live a secret life. He did not veil his actions or hide the details of his ministry. His helper Tychicus knew the details of his affairs enough to make a full report. Paul's transparency did not stop with Tychicus. Onesimus, the converted slave we read about in Paul's letter to Philemon, knew him well too. And, in 1 Thessalonians 2:7–8, Paul wrote of imparting (sharing) his very life with the church in Thessalonica. Paul's life was an open book to that church.

Read Colossians 4:10–14. How many names of friends and associates does Paul list?

_____

Can you name at least two people outside your family circle who hold you accountable and encourage you in your growth in Christ? If not, list people who might be possibilities, people who you would like to establish such a relationship with.

1._____

2._____

The people who served with Paul were deeply aware of his life because he lived it openly in front of them. When we live in community with other believers—as we do with a church—and let others see our strengths and our struggles, we are encouraged to grow. On the other hand, if we are not accountable for our behavior, we often expose ourselves to dangers such as unhealthy obsessions, unchecked habits, unwise relationships, or unrevealed motives.

Does embracing accountability mean we must give up our privacy? Not at all. We all have areas of our lives that are too personal to share. However, accountability is necessary if we are to maintain a strong morality, guard the purity of our ethics, and protect our integrity. Every believer should cultivate a small group of two or three people to whom he or she is accountable.

Likewise, when we look for a church, we should seek out a fellowship where accountability applies not only to the leadership but to every member. When we start a church, we should build accountability into its constitution and bylaws. As with the value of excellence, God's name and reputation are at stake. If we truly seek to honor God, we will cultivate an attitude of openness in our lives that will both protect us from temptation and encourage us to grow spiritually. We will value accountability.

Proverbs 27:6 reads, "Faithful are the wounds of a friend, / But deceitful are the kisses of an enemy." Notice the paradox. The proverb advises us to receive a wound from a friend and reject a kiss from an enemy. Clearly, the rebuke of someone who loves us is no injury.

What do you think Proverbs 27:6 means when it describes the wounds of a friend as faithful?

_____

_____

_____

Do you receive criticism from friends with the same attitude as you receive their praise? Explain.

_____

_____

_____

Do you love your friends enough to offer them faithful wounds that will help them grow, or do you find it more comfortable to stay quiet so you won't hurt their feelings?

_____

_____

If you avoid confrontation by staying quiet, how might your silence hurt your friends?

_____

_____

If we have never invited a few people to tell us the candid truth, we are missing an essential element of the Christian life. Accountability brings responsibility, freedom, encouragement, honesty, and authentic camaraderie into our lives. We know we are loved when people who see all of our junk love us unconditionally and care enough to help us clean it up.

Glory to Our God

In the previous chapters, we discussed five core values that all of us must embrace as we follow Christ: developing greater character in ourselves, extending honor to others, offering grace to people, pursuing excellence in all we do, and embracing accountability with others. Ultimately, all of these point to the sixth value. Our greatest purpose and joy should be *to bring glory to God*. First Corinthians 10:31 reads, "Whether, then, you eat or drink or whatever you do, do all to the glory of God." But what does it mean, "to give God glory?" After all, doesn't He already have all things, glory included?

Simply put, glory involves giving credit to another. When applied to God, glorifying means magnifying, exalting, or uplifting Him while submitting to His authority. John the Baptist says it best: "He must increase, but I must decrease" (John 3:30). Now that's giving God the glory!

Why must we value God's glory? Perhaps because God Himself values His glory. All things everywhere exist to bring glory to God. Paul explains in Romans 11:36, "For from Him and through Him and to Him are all things. To Him be the glory forever. Amen." In other words, glory is all about God—not about us.

No matter what gifts, talents, abilities, or resources we may have, we received them from God, and we are to use them to bring glory and honor to Him. In the words of 1 Peter 4:10:

> As each one has received a special gift, employ it in serving one another as good stewards of the manifold grace of God.

As we use our gifts to build up the body, the credit for those gifts goes to God because He gave them to us. Without His gifts, we would have nothing.

The chief end of humankind is bringing glory to God. Therefore, we do everything with excellence, embrace accountability, cultivate character, and honor others. And when grace reigns supreme, God receives glory!

Are you looking for a church? When you visit, look closely at who receives glory. Is it the pastor? The leaders? The soloist? Do you see a congregation building its own kingdom on earth? Or do you see a body of people committed to Christ, offering every part of their lives as a declaration of God's glory to a watching world? That's a church worth starting or attending. Such people are authentic ambassadors for Christ.

＋—·—＋

> Everything comes from him;
> Everything happens through him;
> Everything ends up in him.
> Always glory! Always praise! Yes. Yes. Yes.
>
> —*Romans 11:36* MSG

HOW TO BEGIN A RELATIONSHIP WITH GOD

Finding or founding a church that is rooted in biblical values includes looking within and looking beyond ourselves. Yet this process must begin with God, who is the Lord of the universe, who knows us better than we know ourselves, and has complete sovereignty not only of our destination in life, but also the steps we take to get there.

If God is the source and center of our lives, how can we come to know Him? How can we be sure our lives are in a right relationship with the only One who knows the end from the beginning and can direct us in the way we should go?

The most marvelous book in the world, the Bible, marks the path to God with four vital truths. Let's look at each marker in detail.

1. *Our Spiritual Condition: Totally Depraved*

The first truth is rather personal. One look in the mirror of Scripture, and our human condition becomes painfully clear:

> There is none righteous, not even one;
> There is none who understands,
> There is none who seeks for God;
> All have turned aside, together they have become useless;
> There is none who does good,
> There is not even one. (Romans 3:10–12)

We are all sinners through and through—totally depraved. Now, that doesn't mean we've committed every atrocity known to humankind. We're not as bad as we can be, just as bad off as we can be. Sin colors all our thoughts, motives, words, and actions.

You still don't believe it? Look around. Everything around us bears the smudge marks of our sinful nature. Despite our best efforts to create a perfect world, crime statistics continue to soar, divorce rates keep climbing, and families keep crumbling.

Something has gone terribly wrong in our society and in ourselves, something deadly. Contrary to how the world would repackage it, "me first" living doesn't equal rugged individuality and freedom; it equals death. As Paul said in his letter the Romans, "The wages of sin is death" (Romans 6:23)—our emotional and physical death through sin's destructiveness, and our spiritual death from God's righteous judgment of our sin. This brings us to the second marker: God's character.

2. *God's Character: Infinitely Holy*

Solomon observed the condition of the world and the people in it and concluded, "Vanity of vanities, all is vanity" (Ecclesiastes 1:2; 12:8). The fact that we know things are not as they should be points us to a standard of goodness beyond ourselves. Our sense of injustice in life implies the existence of a perfect standard of justice. That standard and source is God Himself. And God's standard of holiness contrasts starkly with our sinful condition.

Scripture says that "God is light, and in Him there is no darkness at all" (1 John 1:5). He is absolutely holy—which creates a problem for us. If He is so pure, how can we who are so impure relate to Him?

Perhaps we could try being better people, try to tilt the balance in favor of our good deeds, or seek out wisdom and knowledge for self-improvement. Throughout history, people have attempted to live up to God's standard by keeping the Ten Commandments or living by their own code of ethics. Unfortunately, no one can come close to satisfying the demands of God's law. J. B. Phillips' translation of Romans 3:20 says, "No man can justify himself before God by a perfect performance of the Law's demands—indeed it is the straight-edge of the Law that shows us how crooked we are."

3. *Our Need: A Substitute*

So here we are, sinners by nature, sinners by choice, trying to pull ourselves up by our own bootstraps and attain a relationship with our holy Creator. But every time we try, we fall flat on our faces. We can't live a good enough life to make up for our sin, because God's standard isn't "good enough"—it's perfection. And we can't make amends for the offense our sin has created without dying for it.

Who can get us out of this mess?

If someone could live perfectly, honoring God's law, and would bear sin's death penalty for us—in our place—then we would be saved from our predicament. But is there such a person? Thankfully, yes!

Meet your substitute—Jesus Christ. He is the One who took death's place for you!

> [God] made [Jesus Christ] who knew no sin to be sin on our behalf, that we might become the righteousness of God in Him. (2 Corinthians 5:21)

4. God's Provision: A Savior

God rescued us by sending His Son, Jesus, to die for our sins on the cross (see 1 John 4:9–10). Jesus was fully human and fully divine (John 1:1, 18), a truth that ensures His understanding of our weaknesses, His power to forgive, and His ability to bridge the gap between God and us (see Romans 5:6–11). In short, we are "justified as a gift by His grace through the redemption which is in Christ Jesus" (Romans 3:24). Two words in this verse bear further explanation: *justified* and *redemption*.

Justification is God's act of mercy, in which He declares believing sinners righteous, while they are still in their sinning state. Justification doesn't mean that God makes us righteous, so that we never sin again, rather that He declares us righteous—much like a judge pardons a guilty criminal. Because Jesus took our sin upon Himself and suffered our judgment on the cross, God forgives our debt and proclaims us PARDONED.

Redemption is God's act of paying the ransom price to release us from our bondage to sin. Held hostage by Satan, we were shackled by the iron chains of sin and death. Like a loving parent whose child has been kidnapped, God willingly paid the ransom for you. And what a price He paid! He gave His only Son to bear our sins—past, present, and future. Jesus's death and resurrection broke our chains and set us free to become children of God (see Romans 6:16–18, 22; Galatians 4:4–7).

Placing Your Faith in Christ

These four truths describe how God has provided a way to Himself through Jesus Christ. Since the price has been paid in full by God, we must respond to His free gift of eternal life with total faith and confidence in Him to save us. We must step forward into the relationship with God that He has prepared for us. We do this not by doing good works or being good people, but by coming to Him just as we are and accepting His justification and redemption by faith.

> For by grace you have been saved through faith; and that not of yourselves, it is the gift of God; not as a result of works, that no one should boast. (Ephesians 2:8–9)

We accept God's gift of salvation simply by placing our faith in Christ alone for the forgiveness of our sins. Would you like to enter a relationship with your Creator by trusting in Christ as your Savior? If so, here's a simple prayer you can use to express your faith:

> Dear God,
>
> I know that my sin has put a barrier between You and me. Thank You for sending Your Son, Jesus, to die in my place. I trust in Jesus alone to forgive my sins, and I accept His gift of eternal life. I ask Jesus to be my personal Savior and the Lord of my life. Thank You. In Jesus's name, amen.

If you've prayed this prayer or one like it and you wish to find out more about knowing God and His plan for you in the Bible, contact us at Insight for Living. You can speak to one of our pastors on staff by calling 972-473-5097. Or you can write to us at the address below. Mark your letter to the Pastoral Ministries Department.

> Pastoral Ministries Department
> Insight for Living
> P.O. Box 269000
> Plano, Texas 75026-9000

Of all the possible legacies you could inherit, God's gift of eternal life is the greatest. Of all the legacies you could leave to those who come after you, none can compare with a life lived by faith in the Son of God, who loved us, and gave Himself for us.

ENDNOTES

CHAPTER 1

1. Richard J. Foster, *Money, Sex, & Power: The Challenge of the Disciplined Life* (New York: Harper & Row, 1985), 178. Used by permission of HarperCollins Publishers.

2. David Otis Fuller, *Spurgeon's Lectures to his Students* (Grand Rapids, Mich.: Zondervan Publishing House, 1945), 281.

CHAPTER 2

1. Howard Hendricks, *A Life of Integrity* (Sisters, Ore.: Multnomah Books, 1997), 206. Used by permission.

CHAPTER 3

1. Stephen Arterburn and Jack Felton, *Toxic Faith* (Nashville: Oliver-Nelson Books, 1991), xiv.

2. Philip Yancey, *What's So Amazing about Grace?* (Grand Rapids, Mich.: Zondervan Publishing House, 1997), 42. Used by permission of the Zondervan Corporation.

CHAPTER 4

1. Gordon Dahl, *Work, Play, and Worship* (Minneapolis, Augsburg Publishing House, 1972), 12.

2. Geoffrey W. Bromiley, *Theological Dictionary of the New Testament: Abridged in One Volume* (Nashville: William B. Eerdmans Publishing Company, 1985), 1347-1350.

BOOKS FOR PROBING FURTHER

We hope the time you spent in the *Church-Family Values* workbook has given you the tools you need to establish a set of essentials and core values that will guide you as you look for a church family or help a church grow. As you set a biblical foundation for your church and for yourself, we encourage you to keep digging into what Scripture says about building a strong church.

Harris, Joshua. *Stop Dating the Church! Fall in Love with the Family of God.* Sisters, Ore.: Multnomah Books, 2003.

Lewis, Robert. *The Church of Irresistible Influence.* Grand Rapids, Mich.: Zondervan, 2001.

Macchia, Stephen A. *Becoming a Healthy Church: Ten Traits of a Vital Ministry.* Grand Rapids, Mich.: Baker Books, 2003.

Macchia, Stephen A. *Becoming a Healthy Disciple: Ten Traits of a Vital Christian.* Grand Rapids, Mich.: Baker Books, 2004.

Malphurs, Aubrey. *Being Leaders: The Nature of Authentic Christian Leadership.* Grand Rapids, Mich.: Baker Books, 1999.

McIntosh, Gary L. *One Church, Four Generations: Understanding and Reaching All Ages in Your Church.* Grand Rapids, Mich.: Baker Books, 2002.

Peterson, Eugene H. *Leap Over a Wall: Earthy Spirituality for Everyday Christians.* San Francisco, Calif.: HarperCollins, 1998.

Piper, John. *Brothers, We Are Not Professionals: A Plea to Pastors for Radical Ministry.* Nashville, Tenn.: Broadman & Holman Publishers, 2002.

Piper, John. *Don't Waste Your Life.* Wheaton, Ill.: Crossway Books, 2003.

Sanders, J. Oswald. *Spiritual Leadership.* Chicago, Ill.: Moody Press, 1994.

Stott, John. *The Beatitudes: Developing Spiritual Character.* Downers Grove: Ill.: InterVarsity Press, 1998.

Whitney, Donald S. *Spiritual Disciplines within the Church.* Chicago, Ill.: Moody Press, 1996.

Wagner, Glen E. and Glen S. Martin. *Your Pastor's Heart: Serving the One Who Serves You.* Chicago, Ill.: Moody Publishers, 1998.

Yancey, Phillip. *Church: Why Bother?* Grand Rapids, Mich.: Zondervan, 1998.

ORDERING INFORMATION

Church-Family Values

If you would like to order additional workbooks, purchase the audio series that accompanies this workbook, or request our product catalog, please contact the office that serves you.

United States and International locations:

Insight for Living
Post Office Box 269000
Plano, TX 75026-9000
1-800-772-8888, 24 hours a day, seven days a week (U.S. contacts)
International constituents may contact the U.S. office through mail queries or call 1-972-473-5136.

Canada:

Insight for Living Ministries
Post Office Box 2510
Vancouver, BC V6B 3W7
1-800-663-7639, 24 hours a day, seven days a week
info@insightcanada.org

Australia:

Insight for Living, Inc.
Suite 4, 43 Railway Road
Blackburn, VIC 3130
AUSTRALIA
Toll-free 1800 772 888 or 61 3 9877 4277, 9:00 A.M. to 5:00 P.M.
Monday through Friday
info@aus.insight.org
www.insight.asn.au

Internet:

www.insight.org

Workbook Subscription Program

Bible study workbook subscriptions are available. Please call or write the office nearest you to find out how you can receive our workbooks on a regular basis.

NOTES

NOTES

NOTES

NOTES